First published in Great Britain in 2004 by
PAST TIMES® Oxford, England
A nice cup of… by Michelle Lovric

Printed in China by Imago

Designed by Michelle Lovric and Lisa Pentreath
Concept, compilation and text copyright
© 2004 Michelle Lovric
Editorial Assistant: Kristina Blagojevitch

9 8 7 6 5 4 3 2 1

WITH THE SEASON'S

HEARTY GREETING

WITH BEST WISHES.

**Michelle Lovric has asserted
her right to be identified as the
author of this work in accordance
with the Copyright, Designs and
Patents Act, 1988.**

**A catalogue record for this book is
available from the British Library.**

With special thanks to Professor Irving Y. Lo

A nice cup of...

WISHING YOU MANY HAPPY RETURNS OF THE DAY

WITH BEST WISHES

Tea, Coffee, Chocolate &
other liquid delights!

Compiled by Michelle Lovric

...Wine and Strong Drink make Tumults encrease,
Chocolate, Tea, and Coffee, are Liquors of Peace;
No Quarrels or Oaths among those that drink them.

Andrew Marvell (1621–78)
English poet

Cont

Introduction

Most of us seek comfort in a nice warm cup of something. Whether in solitude or company, whether reading or chatting, we automatically pour ourselves something hot to lubricate both the mouth and the brain. The drinks that we choose are mild stimulants, tea, coffee and chocolate, full of flavour and perfumed not just with their own essence but also cultural and emotional resonances. Western society makes a ritual of these drinks, and the advertising industry has always been quick to take advantage of the exotic and romantic aspects of their origin and manufacture.

Some of the most beautiful, alluring and extravagant advertisements ever produced have been inspired by these drinks. When colour printing first became an economically viable possibility in the nineteenth century, the beverage industry was one of the first to make use of it. All kinds of colourful, witty and ingenious advertisements were produced.

This book combines quotations about tea, coffee and hot chocolate with three-dimensional examples of some of the most enjoyable paper-engineered trade cards to advertise them. There are teacups that reveal how to read one's fortune in the leaves. There are cards that open up to tell a story with a changing picture. There are cards die-cut in the shape of cups and printed on both sides, pop-up cards, and 'metamorphs' that deliver a surprise.

Find yourself a cup; the teapot is behind you. Now tell me about hundreds of things.

Saki (Hector Hugo Munro) (1870–1916)
British writer

Znts

Goutez et comparez

Qualité sans Rivale.

CHOC

Las cosas claras y el chocolate espeso. (Ideas should be clear and chocolate thick.)

Spanish proverb

'Tis pity wine should be so deleterious,
For tea and coffee leave us much more serious ...

George Gordon, Lord Byron (1788–1824)
English poet

5

The tea in fragrant fumes ascends,
The sister coffee too attends ...

William Combe (1742–1823)
English poet

Tea

Thank God for tea!
What would the world
do without tea! How did
it exist? I am glad I was
not born before tea.

Sydney Smith (1771–1845)
English clergyman and essayist

Tea! thou soft, thou sober, sage and venerable liquid ...
thou female tongue-running, smile-smoothing, heart-opening,
wink-tippling cordial, to whose glorious insipidity I owe the
happiest moment of my life, let me fall prostrate.

Colley Cibber (1671–1757)
English actor and dramatist

Tea ... is a religion of the art of life.

Kakuzo Okakura (1862–1913)
Japanese writer

Its liquor is like the sweetest dew from Heaven.

Lu Yu (733–804)
Chinese writer

Better to be deprived of food for three days than tea for one.

We drank our tea in China beneath the sacred spice-trees,
And heard the curled waves of the harbour moan.

Vachel Lindsay (1879–1931)
American poet

Each cup of tea

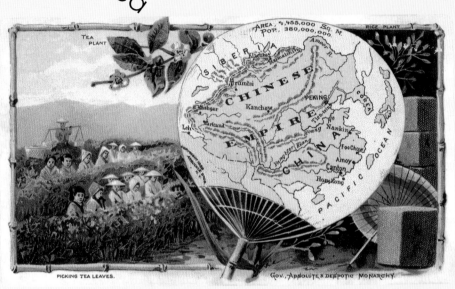

PICKING TEA LEAVES.   Gov., Absolute & Despotic Monarchy.

On a cold night when the guests arrive, I
serve tea instead of wine;
O'er a bamboo brazier, water starts
to boil and the fire glows red.

Anonymous Chinese poet,
translated by Irving Yucheng Lo

represen

I sent for a cup of tee – a China drink– of which I had never drank before

Samuel Pepys (1633–1703)
English diarist

8

The best quality tea must have creases like the leather boot of Tartar horsemen, curl like the dewlap of the mighty bullock, unfold like mist rising out a ravine ...

Lu Yu (733–804)
Chinese writer

In praise of Bamboo Brazier:
The Prince of Bitter Integrity – An Encomium

Shaped to resemble Heaven and Earth,
But not made either of clay or metal;
A live fire in its belly,
Its sound echoes the waves of River Hsaing.
Just one drop of its sweet dew
Cleanses all my innards for poetry.
Then pure breeze rises from beneath my armpits,
And I can see everything clear to the world's end.

Lu T'ing-ts'an, Chinese poet,
translated by Irving Yucheng Lo

9

Catherine Donzel
Contemporary French writer

n imaginary voyage.

There is a great deal of poetry and fine sentiment in a chest of tea.

Ralph Waldo Emerson (1803–82)
American poet and essayist

The distinctive feature of **MOORE BROS'** System is that they supply FAMILIES DIRECT at MERCHANTS' PRICES for Cash £3 value, carriage paid.

On the Virtues of Tea

The particular virtues are these; it maketh the body active and lusty; it helpeth the headache, giddiness and heaviness thereof; it removeth the obstructiveness of the Spleen; it is very good against the stone and gravel, cleaning the kidneys and ureters, being drank with virgin's honey, instead of sugar; it taketh away the difficulty of breathing, opening obstructions; it is good against tipitude, distillations, and cleareth the sight; it removeth lassitude and cleanseth and purifieth acrid humours and a hot liver ... it vanquisheth heavy dreames, easeth the frame and strengtheneth the memory; it overcometh superfluous sleep, and prevents sleepiness in general ...

Handbill of Thomas Garway, tobacconist and tea merchant, London, 1667

It is very strange, this domination
of our intellect by our digestive
organs. We cannot work, we cannot
think, unless our stomach wills so.
It dictates to us our emotions, our
passions. After eggs and bacon it
says, 'Work!' After beefsteak and
porter, it says, 'Sleep!' After a cup
of tea (two spoonfuls for each cup,
and don't let it stand for more than
three minutes), it says to the brain,
'Now rise, and show your strength.
Be eloquent, and deep, and tender;
see, with a clear eye, into Nature, and
into life: spread your white
wings of quivering thought,
and soar, a
god-like spirit, over
the whirling world
beneath you, up
through long lanes
of flaming stars
to the gates of
eternity!'

Jerome K. Jerome (1859–1927)
English writer

[I am] a hardened and shameless tea-drinker, who has, for twenty years, diluted his meals with only the infusion of this fascinating plant; whose kettle has scarcely time to cool; who with tea amuses the evening, with tea solaces the midnight, and, with tea, welcomes the morning.

Samuel Johnson (1709–84)
English writer and lexicographer

Johnson's biographer, Boswell, supposed that 'no person ever enjoyed with more relish the infusion of that fragrant leaf ... the quantities he drank at all hours were so great, that his nerves must have been uncommonly strong not to have been extremely relaxed by such intemperate use of it; but he assured me he never felt the least inconvenience from it.'

12

What part of confidante has that poor teapot played ever since the kindly plant was introduced among us! Why myriads of women have cried over it, to be sure! What sickbeds it has smoked by! What fevered lips have received refreshment from it! Nature meant very kindly by women when she made the tea plant; and with a little thought, what a series of pictures and groups the fancy may conjure up and assemble round the teapot and cup.

William Makepeace Thackeray (1811–63)
English novelist

Tea, though ridiculed by those who are naturally coarse in their nervous sensibilities – will always be the favourite beverage of the intellectual.

Thomas De Quincy (1785–1859)
English critic and essayist

And when the brown seer her wonderful cup,
With thick-settled tea-leaves, had whirled and turned up,
I deemed, as she looked so sagacious within it,
The end of my being was fixed from that minute;
That if the least specks on its sides were deranged,
'Twas over – my fortune forever was changed!
With motion suspended, and speech wholly gone,
In wonder and awe, as I stood and looked on ...

YOUR FORTUNE IN THE TEA-CUP

If your fate you want to know,
What's in store this cup will show;

Within it you will find a key
To read the Future's mystery. 1164

... The thread of my life at that moment seemed hung,
In its many-hued twist, from the tip of her tongue.
And she opened her lips with such bright and fair things,
That, my head all on fire, and my fancy on wings,
I flew to my home, and retired to my bed,
To gild my gay dreamings with all she had said.

Hannah Gould (1789–1865)
American poet

15

Polly put the kettle on,
Polly put the kettle on,
Polly put the kettle on,
We'll all have tea.

16

Now stir the fire, and close the shutters fast,

Let fall the curtains, wheel the sofa round,

And, while the bubbling and loud hissing urn

Throws up a steamy column, and the cups

That cheer but not inebriate, wait on each,

So let us welcome peaceful ev'ning in.

William Cowper (1731–1800)
English poet

Henry James (1843–1916)
American writer

... And your pretty playthings

Of china saucers, with their fairy cups,

In which a wren could scarcely lay her egg, –

Your tea-pot, pouring from its slender beak

Hot water, as it were some precious drug,

Must be, for fashion's sake, set in array

To please the Lowland lady.

Joanna Baillie (1762–1851)
Scottish dramatist and poet

17

Wilkie Collins (1824–89)
English novelist

A Nice Cup of Tea
AT
Harrogate

18

They may talk of the ruin
That Bacchus is brewing,
But if my advice a young soldier would ask, sir,
I would say that the hiccups
Are safer than tea-cups,
So beware of the *chaynee* and stick to your flask, sir.
Had I stood to my bowl,
Like a gay jovial soul,
By this time I might be a general officer;
But I dallied with Sally,
And Betty, and Ally,
And lost all my time with their *tay* and their coffee, sir –
Oh! *tay* is a dangerous drink,
When the lady that makes it's a beauty;
With her fingers so *nate*
She presents you a plate,
And to cut bread and butter she puts you on duty;
Then she pouts her bright lips,
While the Congou she sips,
And her sweet mouth some question demanding,
Puts your heart beyond all self-commanding,
Through the steam of the teapot her eyes shine like stars,
And Venus again makes a conquest of Mars.

Samuel Lover (1797–1868)
Irish writer and artist

ut if this is tea, please bring me some coffee.

Abraham Lincoln (1809–65)
American president

19

Love and scandal
are the best sweeteners of tea.

Henry Fielding (1707–54)
English novelist

coffee

20

Every care vanishes when the cup bearer presents thee the
delicious chalice. It will circulate fleetly through thy veins ...

Sheik Abdal-Kader Anasari Djezeri Haubali
Sixteenth-century Arab writer

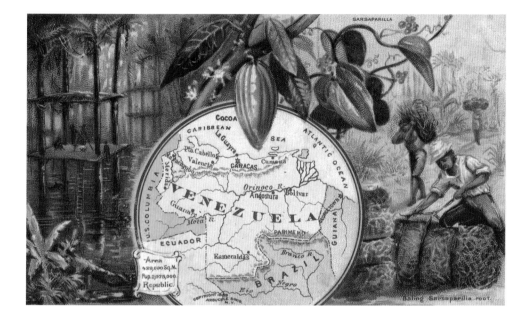

And then the coffee, with its amber shine,
In aromatic richness half divine –
Brought Araby, and Araby the 'Nights'.

John Critchley Prince (1808–66)
English poet

Ah! How sweet coffe

Lovelier than

Delicious berry, but, ah! best
When from the Eastern Ind, not West;
Nought richer is, I think, than *thee*: –
Into a roaster, with my hand,
I put thee, and then o'er thee stand,
And then I catch thy smell with glee.

And now I shake thee round about;
And, when turn'd brown, I take thee out,
And then I put thee in a mill;
And, when to powder thou art crush'd,
Into a tin pot thou art push'd,
To feel the boiling smoking rill.

And now from my tin pot's long nose
The fragrant fluid sweetly flows;
And now I put the lily cream,
And sugar too, the best of brown;
And, happy, now I gulp thee down
Keeping my nose upon the steam.

Peter Pindar (John Wolcot) (1738–1819)
English poet and satirist

stes!

ousand kisses,

sweeter far than muscatel wine!

Johann Sebastian Bach
(1685–1750)
German composer

Bach wrote his comic 'Coffee Cantata',
also known as 'Be Quiet, Stop Talking', with
the middle-class clientele of Leipzig's coffee
houses in mind. It tells the story of a young
girl's addiction to coffee and her father's
attempts to help her give it up.

Ah, that is a perfume
in which I delight;
when they roast coffee
near my house, I hasten
to open the door to take
in all the aroma.

Jean Jacques Rousseau (1712–78)
French writer and philosopher

The powers of a man's mind are directly proportional
to the quantity of coffee he drank.

Sir James MacKintosh (1765–1832)
English philosopher

24

O Coffee!

Thou dispellest the cares of the great; thou bringest back those who
wander from the paths of knowledge. Coffee is the beverage of the
people of God, and the cordial of his servants who thirst for wisdom.
When coffee is infused into the bowl, it exhales the odour of musk,
and is the colour of ink. The truth is not known except to the wise
who drink it from the foaming coffee cup.

Sheik Abdal-Kader Anasari Djezeri Haubali
Sixteenth-century Arab writer

rink coffee; it is the intelligent beverage.

A cup of coffee – real coffee – home-browned,
home-ground, home-made, that comes to
you dark as a hazel-eye, but changes to a
golden bronze as you temper it with cream
that never cheated, but was real cream
from its birth, thick, tenderly yellow,
perfectly sweet, neither lumpy not frothing
on the java: such a cup of coffee is a match
for twenty blue devils and will exorcise them all.

Henry Ward Beecher
Ameri...

Coffee is real good when you drink it, it gives you time to think.
It's a lot more than just a drink; it's something happening. Not as
in hip, but like an event, a place to be, but not like a location,
but like somewhere within yourself. It gives you time, but not
actual hours or minutes, but a chance to be, like be yourself,
and have a second cup.

Gertrude Stein (1874–1946)
American writer

25

Sydney Smith (1771–1845)
English clergyman and essayist

The morning cup of coffee has
an exhilaration about it which the
cheering influence of the afternoon
or evening cup of tea cannot be
expected to reproduce.

Oliver Wendell Holmes (1809–94)
American writer

Coffee glides down into one's stomach and ...
one's ideas advance in columns of route
like battalions of the Grande Armée

Honoré de Balzac (1799–1850)
French writer

Without my morning coffee I'm just like
a dried-up piece of roast goat.

Johann Sebastian Bach (1685–1750)
German composer

The first cup is for the guest,
the second for enjoyment,
the third for the sword.

Arabic saying

... a pot

Of sage-inspiring coffee ...

Mark Akenside (1721–70)
English poet

The coffee is prepared in such a way that it makes those who drink it witty: at least there is not a single soul who, on quitting the house, does not believe himself four times wittier that when he entered it.

Charles de Secondat Montesquieu (1689–1755)
French philosopher and jurist

Coffee works a miracle, sharpening the brains of the stupid. No author refreshed thereby need languish in silence. Coffee's strength and virtue double the memory. Every drop empowers us to gabble without pause, and, discarding the crutches of rhyme, to spout fable as history.

Anonymous eighteenth-century writer

On Coffee

As long as Moco's happy tree shall grow,

While Berries crackle, or while Mills shall go;

While smoking Streams from Silver Spouts shall glide,

Or China's Earth receive the sable Tyde;

While Coffee shall to British Nymphs be dear;

While fragrant Steams the bended Head shall chear;

Or grateful Bitters shall delight the Tast;

So long her Honour, Name, and Praise shall last!

Alexander Pope (1688–1744)
English poet

The Seasons Greeting

Suave molecules of Mocha stir up your blood, without causing
excess heat; the organ of thought receives from it a feeling of
sympathy; work becomes easier and you will sit down without
distress to your principal repast which will restore your body
and afford you a calm, delicious night.

Charles Maurice de Talleyrand-Périgord (1754–1839)
French statesman

Coffee should be black as hell, strong as death and sweet as love.

Turkish proverb

CHOCOLATE

32

The fruit is like almonds,

lying in a shell resembling a gourd in size. It ripens in a year, and being plucked when the season has arrived, they pick out the kernels and lay them on the mats to dry; then when they wish for the beverage, they roast them in an earthen pan over the fire, and grind them ... Finally, they put the paste into cups ... and mixing it gradually with water, sometimes adding a little of their spice, they drink it ... I was upwards of a year in that country without ever being induced to taste this beverage, and when I passed through a tribe, if an Indian wished occasionally to give me some, he was very much surprised to see me refuse it and went away laughing.

Girolamo Benzoni (1519–?)
Milanese traveller and writer, describing cocoa beans

I always drink *Huyler's* Cocoa or Chocolate!

CHOCOLATE

Sonnet in Praise of Hot Chocolate

Let it never be said that,
before going to bed,
I don't put my right
And my left hand together
without saying a requiem
for that good Christian
whose family gave him
the name Columbus.
Not just because he found
pure silver and gold,
because for me he did
that in vain;

Not because he conquered lands
for the Spanish king –
since I'm not so fond
of the Spanish myself;
But simply because he brought
from the new world
the sweet blessed potion
that we call Chocolate.
And for that I feel a
greater devotion than
have the Certosine Friars
for their wine-drenched fry-ups.
It has no beginning or end,
this love that I have for the
daughter of cocoa,
cinnamon, sugar and vanilla;
I would go three hundred miles
barefoot just to drink a
little cup of it,
I would pawn my Breviary
and my robe.
Truly my guts
are (And I wouldn't like to tell you
any wickedness) for chocolate
like a pig's lusting after acorns.
I would give up all beverages –
I would give up tocai, and malvasia –
and the whole genealogy of wines:
If I could only be given
that holy liquor which
touches my heart,
which only to name it

makes my mouth water.
But there are lots of idiots
who believe that the Gods' ambrosia
would be a better drink than chocolate ...
He who never tries it could not believe
how many blessings it has for us,
delivering us first of all from all evils,
apart from death ...
My soul, dead and buried;
will go begging, that my flesh,
turning under the earth
till it becomes earthenware,
shall not be made into plates or urinals
but instead into little royal cups
for holding Chocolate
So that after death
I shall be still in my beatitude.

Antonio Sforza
Eighteenth-century Italian writer

35

If you

are not

feeling well,

if you

have not

slept,

chocolate

will revive

you.

But you

have no

chocolate!

I think

of that

again

and again!

36

MILL
ESTABLISHED
1828.

SPIN THE ARMS ROUND QUICKLY AND GAZE AT CENTRE.

VAN
HOUTEN'S
COCOA.

My dear, how will you eve

It's not that chocolates
are a substitute for love.
Love is a substitute
for chocolate.
Chocolate is, let's face it,
far more reliable than a man.

Miranda Ingram
Contemporary writer

Fruit of all the kinds that the country produced were laid before him; he ate very little, but from time to time a liquor prepared from cocoa, and of an aphrodisiac nature, as we were told, was presented to him in golden cups ...
I observed a number of jars, above fifty, brought in, filled with foaming chocolate, of which he took some ...

Bernal Diaz del Castillo (1492–1584)
Spanish soldier and historian, describing a meal of the Mexican Emperor Montezuma

'Twill make old women Young and Fresh;
Create new notions of the flesh
And cause them long for you know what,
If they but taste of chocolate

James Wadsworth (1768–1844)
American writer

One frosty afternoon in 1760,

the dashing young hero commands his chaise to stop before this quaint chocolate shop, first of its kind in Vienna. He must discover for himself the merits of a rich new beverage ... that romantic drink from the tropics which is the topic of conversation among all the young fashionables.

He enters, seats himself at a table, orders 'hot chocolate' and promptly discovers not only the glories of this mellow, fragrant drink, but also the prettiest girl in all Vienna.

Day after day, he returns for more chocolate and more demure glances. The bewildering enchantment grows and grows ... until his daily cup of chocolate becomes the most important event in Prince Ditrichstein's life. He completely forgets that a Prince may not look at a waitress ... And the rest you've already guessed!

As a betrothal gift, Ditrichstein engaged a talented Swiss artist, Jean Etienne Liotard, to paint his winsome beloved in the simple costume in which she first bewitched him. This portrait now hangs in the Dresden Museum ... and its well-known replica graces every can of Walter Baker's Breakfast Cocoa.

From *Best Chocolate and Cocoa Recipes*, published by Baker's, the manufacturers

42

... The nymph who sups upon quadrille and tea,
In sleep, affected by the cogent streams,
Of full canals, and falling waters dreams;
If sullen coffee close the sober night,
Dark walls, and abby-grates amuse the sight;
But dreams of most import (if late apply'd)
In chocolate's productive fumes reside ...

Joseph Thurston (fl. 1730)
English poet

Cadbury's

CADBURY'S

"No Better Food." Dr. Andrew Wilson, F.R.S.E., &c.

"My IDEAL of PERFECTION" Dr. Andrew Wilson F.R.S.E.

"When the heart of a man"   "The mist is dispelled"
"Is o'er clouded with fears;"   "When a woman appears"
With a cup of FRY'S COCOA to cheer him.

Fry's **PURE CONCENTRATED**

300 Gold Medals, &c.   **Cocoa**

N.B.—Sold only in tins with gilt tops.

Chocolate is a perfect food, as wholesome as it is delicious,
a beneficent restorer of exhausted power.
It is the best friend of those engaged in literary pursuits.

Baron Justus von Liebig (1803–73)
German chemist

If any man has drunk a little too deeply from the cup of physical pleasure; if he has spent too much time at his desk that should have been spent asleep; if his fine spirits have become temporarily dulled; if he finds the air too damp, the minutes too slow, and the atmosphere too heavy to withstand; if he is obsessed by a fixed idea which bars him from any freedom of thought: if he is any of these poor creatures, we say, let him be given a good pint of amber-flavoured chocolate ... and marvels will be performed.

Anthelme Brillat-Savarin (1755–1826)
French politician and writer

He took his chocolate liberally, pouring in larg

uantities of cream, or even melted butter.

Hester Thrale (1741–1821), English writer, on her friend Samuel Johnson

A GOOD ANGEL'S VISIT.
A TALE OF SCOVILL'S SARSAPARILLA
OR BLOOD & LIVER SYRUP.

NOW EVERY TRACE OF SCROFULA HAS DISAPPEARED,
HER FACE, EVER MARRED BY BLOTCHES, WHICH SHE FEARED
WOULD NEVER GO AWAY, IS FAIR ONCE MORE
AND BRIGHTER, HANDSOMER THAN EVER BEFORE.
FOR ALL DISEASES OF THE BLOOD AND LIVER,
SOMETHING FROM THEIR FURY TO DELIVER-
OR FOR A PLEASANT TONIC, ALL YOUR BLOOD TO STIR UP,
TAKE SCOVILL'S SARSAPARILLA OR BLOOD AND LIVER SYRUP.

Tea, coffee and chocolate have long had their rivals, in the form of 'restorative' syrups and tonics that were heavily advertised, particularly during the Victorian period. Their names were often picturesque and their marvels were told in little stories and scenarios depicted on trade cards. The public were intrigued by drinks sold under titles such as Ramsey's Trinidad Aromatic Bitters, Dr Crook's Compound Syrup of Poke Root, Wistar's Balsam of Wild Cherry and Forni's Alpenkrauter Blutbeleber. Many of these had a high alcohol content. Also popular, and much more innocuous, were hot drinks extracted from beef or vegetables.

Other...

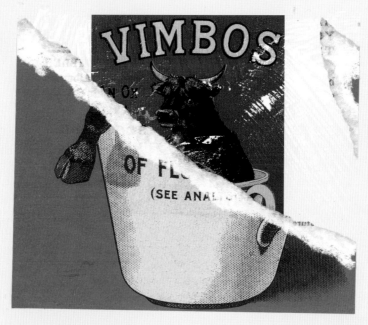

Liquid
Delights

Beef Tea Made with ARMOUR'S Extract of Beef is a delicious drink for the dyspeptic, or any one with a weak stomach. It is easy to make; economical, and a most excellent tonic.

Good Soups & Sauces are not difficult to make if properly combined with stock made from Armour's Extract of Beef. Directions with each Jar. Sold by all Druggists & Grocers

Armour & Company, Chicago.

She's as strong as an ox.
She'll be turned into Bovril when she dies.

Margot Asquith (1864–1945)
English writer, on Lady Desborough

Life is a cup of tea;
the more heartily we drink
the sooner we reach the dregs.

James Matthew Barrie (1860–1937)
Scottish writer